Con trick to start a religion?

A WOMAN has been asked out by the man of her dreams. He is handsome, charming, strong and considerate. He has hired a box at the theatre and greets her with a single red rose and a heart-shaped box of chocolates bearing her name in gold-leaf letters. They hold hands throughout the performance and, during the interval, he presents her with a small jewellery box. She opens it and pulls out a long, delicate silver chain. Her wide-eyed pleasure quickly turns to open-mouthed confusion when she realises that on the end of the chain is a replica electric chair depicting a man being electrocuted. Far from being the man of her dreams, maybe he is the madman of her nightmares.

It's interesting to note that although she recoils at the replica electric chair, she would have been charmed if she had found a crucifix at the end of the chain. Romantic men have been presenting little silver crosses to their girlfriends for as long as they have been booking seats at the theatre. But such sentimental thinking reveals a profound misunderstanding about Jesus' death on a cross.

Moses, Muhammad and Buddha

You sometimes hear people say that the origin of all religions is the same: a person with great moral, spiritual and intellectual standing gains a new insight of truth and dedicates his life to teaching that truth. He then builds a culture around it which outlasts him and guarantees the future of his creed.

As far as Judaism, Buddhism and Islam are concerned, there is some credibility in that analysis, because these religions did begin in this way. Moses, the Buddha and Muhammad died as old men after a life of teaching in which they won vast popular acclaim. For them, the future of their respective religions was guaranteed.

The origin of Christianity cannot be explained in this way, however, because

Jesus died aged 33 after a teaching ministry of three years at most. He had been rejected by society, betrayed and denied by his own supporters, mocked by his enemies, and, at the very end, abandoned by all except his mum and a few of her friends. Jesus suffered one of the most brutal forms of execution ever devised. The founder of Christianity died prematurely and tragically as a lonely, pathetic figure on a cross, yet Jesus has millions more followers than anyone else, alive or dead.

WHY did Jesus die?

One possible explanation for Jesus' death on a cross is that he got carried away with events and didn't see it coming. The weakness of that is that Jesus knew that his life was heading towards a brutal death in Jerusalem. He knew exactly when his time had come and what it entailed.

If you read John's eyewitness biography of Jesus' life (the Gospel of John), you will notice that throughout it Jesus talks of "his hour" – the hour in which he will be glorified. Early in his ministry, Jesus' friends and family urged him to reveal his authority and power. When asked to perform a miracle at a large wedding feast, Jesus responded, "My hour has not yet come" (John 2:4, NIV). By chapter 12 we find ourselves in the last week of Jesus' life. Jesus says, "The hour has come for the Son of Man to be glorified," (verse 23, NIV). This is the big moment: the turning point in John's account. Until then, no one knew what Jesus meant by "his hour". This is an incredibly tense and devastating time, especially for Jesus' closest followers and family. A few verses on, Jesus says: "Now my heart is troubled, and what shall I say? 'Father, save me from this hour'? No, it was for this very reason I came to this hour" (verse 27, NIV). And just in case we are in any doubt about what Jesus means, he continues: "'And I, when I am lifted up from the earth, will draw all people to myself.' He said this to show the kind of death he was going to die" (verses 32-33, NIV).

A murder most foul

Jesus deliberately went to the cross. This was his hour, the hour he had planned for and was born to fulfil. But doesn't it strike you as unusual that Jesus — having spent three years in public ministry in which he demonstrated his authority over sickness, nature and evil, and having convinced his followers that he is God in human form — would then end his life so violently, deliberately and humiliatingly?

Why does the Old Testament look forward to his death, and the New Testament look back on it, as the greatest event in world history? Why is the most significant person in world history deliberately moving events towards his own brutal execution? Surely, it is not going to help anyone, except his enemies.

Hardened soldiers arrested Jesus, blindfolded him, punched him in the face and mocked him: "Hey, you're a prophet – tell us which one of us punched you – come on prophesy, Jesus!" Having been beaten up and had his back flogged, Jesus was then forced to carry his own cross, staggering through the streets, until he arrived at the place of execution. He was stripped naked by rough, sneering soldiers and then thrown onto the cross; his arms and legs were stretched out and surrendered to cruel nails. The cross was then lifted up and dropped into a deep socket, dislocating both his arms as it landed with a judder in its earthen socket. Then, as Jesus began slowly to suffocate in his own blood and spittle, howls of mockery went up from the crowd (see Matthew 27:40-43):

"He saved others, but he can't save himself!"

"Hey, get down from the cross if you really are who you say you are."

Here is the greatest figure the world has ever seen. The one who gave sight to the blind and stilled a storm with a word. The one who convinced John that he was God in human form, the *Logos*, the meaning behind the universe, here he is dying so horribly and deliberately at the hands of his own creation. The whole thing seems obscene not least because it was so avoidable.

Jesus didn't need to keep Judas Iscariot in his company; he had detected his treachery early enough not to trust him. Neither did Jesus need to walk unprotected into an obvious political trap: Jesus was fully aware of what was unfolding around him, and deliberately moved events towards his own execution.

A demonstration of love

Early in John's Gospel we read: **"God loved the world so much that he gave his one and only Son to die"** (see 3:16). Well, if the gift of Jesus was meant to be a demonstration of love to the world, then why did Jesus allow evil to win the day? Why did he cause his widowed mother so much pain and anguish? Would she have been impressed by this entirely avoidable act of sacrifice?

Can you imagine the circumstances in which you blew your own brains out with a gun in front of your mother and in so doing persuaded her that you had performed a noble and loving act? Or imagine a man taking his wife on a long romantic walk by a riverbank. He proposes his undying love to her before throwing himself into the raging current, never to surface again. Would she be comforted by his dying words: "I love you so much – that's why I am doing this"? I doubt she would see how the loving and the dying are connected any more than your mother would after witnessing your own barbaric self-slaughter. She would surely have expected her husband to show his love by living for her, protecting her from loneliness and grief, not by breaking her heart and leaving her bereft.

Seen in its immediate context, the death of Jesus on the cross looks like an extravagant, self-indulgent and cruel miscalculation. Jesus' disciples certainly thought so as they fled for their lives. Yet within a few weeks, the same people claimed that Jesus' death was the greatest hour of his life, his moment of glory, and the most supreme demonstration of love ever shown. So what, then, is the meaning of Jesus' death?

Jesus defeated?

After the battle of Waterloo, English troops received this message: "Wellington defeated". They were utterly dejected and humiliated by the announcement of a French victory. But as they prepared to flee back to England, someone cried out, "We haven't got the full message", so they looked again and realised the full message was "Wellington defeated Napoleon". Upon receiving the initial message "Jesus defeated", the disciples fled the scene of his execution, humiliated and shamed and unable to show themselves in public, but within a few weeks they were boldly proclaiming "Jesus defeated sin and death and hell."

Sin and death are the two greatest enemies of all time, for they have defeated the dreams and aspirations of everyone who has ever walked this planet. Do you have a solution to death and to the sin that blights your life and makes you guilty before a just and blameless God? Ever since humans rebelled against God, we have forfeited the right to eternal life. God will not permit proud, selfish, rebellious people to live for ever; we would only corrupt and destroy a new paradise in our unchanged rebellious condition.

"I made you," says God, "I made a world for you to live in and yet you live as if I didn't exist and you have made a rubbish tip of paradise." It's not very flattering, but we have to wake up to the fact that we are rebellious and sinful and that we greatly offend God. All of us will die because of sin entering God's world and all of us naturally face the punishment of being separated from him for ever, which is an appalling prospect. If God is the source of love, beauty, kindness and goodness, to be separated from him for ever is to be without everything that makes life meaningful.

The hardest thing for God

God spent centuries teaching Israel that he is unapproachably holy. He ordered a mobile temple (tabernacle) to be built that presented itself as an obstacle course. It was full of holy things and had thick musty curtains that you could only go through after ceremonial washings and other strictly prescribed rituals. The message was stark: "God is holy. Proceed with extreme caution or keep out."

It's a bit like *Harry Potter and the Philosopher's Stone*: even if you can get past the three-headed dog, you've still got to avoid the deadly potions and not be killed by the living chess pieces which will smash you down the moment you make a false move.

Why can't God just forgive people?

As I go around universities speaking to students, I constantly hear people ask: "Why doesn't God just forgive people?" As Catherine the Great is reputed to have said, "We sin. God forgives. Forgiveness is his business." No, God's business is not simply to forgive sin. His business is to be true to himself and his just character and so uphold his righteous rule in the universe, to make sure justice is upheld and his just name and rule are honoured.

In the Old Testament, the priests entered the outer room (the Holy Place) to carry out their relentless ministry of sacrificing animals, because "Without the shedding of blood there is no forgiveness" (Hebrews 9:22, NIV). Only the high priest could enter the Most Holy Place, and even then only once a year after making sacrifices for his own sin and the sin of the people. If we are to comprehend why forgiveness is so difficult, and why Jesus had to die as our substitute, we must grasp something of God's holiness and majesty.

This is why forgiveness is such a big problem. How can we be forgiven without God's goodness and essential justice being compromised? What would we think of a judge who unilaterally pronounced forgiveness on a serial rapist who had abducted and tortured young girls on the grounds that he was moved by the rapist's personal circumstances and wanted to express sympathy by granting him an unqualified pardon?

Would God be good if he was merely pained by our sin? If God is not filled with wrath and righteous indignation, how can he possibly be good, holy and just?

Gary Haugen (former Director of the UN genocide investigation in Rwanda) said:

"Standing with my boots deep in the reeking muck of a Rwandan mass grave where thousands of innocent people have been horribly slaughtered, I have no words, no meaning, no life, no hope if there is not a God of history and time who is absolutely furious, absolutely burning with anger towards those who took it in their own hands to commit such acts."

God must punish wrongdoing

God must punish wrongdoing in his universe, because he can never overlook sin. Sin is a rejection of God and his rule and is the cause of all the desperate misery in this world. A just and holy God is rightly angry at sin and demands justice. If we have a problem with that, then we would have an even bigger problem with a God who remained serene in the face of evil and rebellion and simply offered forgiveness with the same sense of duty as Santa Claus offering presents to children.

How can we expect God to be indifferent to our rebellion, pride and ingratitude towards him? Our thoughts and motives are so foul and rebellious, our selfishness and bitterness is so obscene to God. He is angry, and if he were not angry, then he would not be good.

We do not understand Jesus' cross because we do not understand our own danger. On the cross, Jesus offered himself to satisfy God's demand for sin to be punished, for justice to be done. Jesus died to save us from God's righteous anger against sin and wickedness. Jesus was taking our place. He took on himself our punishment. Why would he do that? Simply out of love. Being angry at our sin did not stop God loving us and planning a rescue: "For God so loved the world that he gave his one and only Son, that whoever believes in him should not perish but have eternal life" (John 3:16, NIV).

Loving and dying revisited

Imagine yourself once again walking into your mother's house: this time you realise she has disturbed an armed robber. The burglar raises his gun to shoot, but you somehow manage to throw yourself in front of your mother so that the bullet goes into you and you take the full impact of the shot. As the burglar flees and your mother watches you die, do you think she will have any difficulty seeing a connection between your self-sacrifice and your love for her?

As for the romantic walk along the riverbank, imagine slightly different circumstances in which the woman has lost her footing and accidentally falls into the raging, icy water. Without any concern for his own safety, the husband jumps in alongside her and pushes her to the safety of the river bank. In so doing, he dooms himself and is swept downstream to his death. Once again, however shocked and distraught she is, the woman will have no difficulty seeing how the loving and dying are connected: he died to save her.

In dying on the cross, Jesus took our bullet; he plunged into the icy river of death in the place of sinful humanity to rescue us from certain and eternal death. Our sin is so serious that for God to be satisfied that sin and evil had been sufficiently punished, it required Jesus, who had committed no sin himself, to die in our place.

The scandal of substitution

Is God really just and fair in attributing our sin to the righteous Jesus and acquitting us?

Surely, that is like the pagan gods being offered innocent children? How can it be fair that God seizes Jesus, who is an innocent bystander, and loads the guilt and punishment for our sin on him? Surely, this should be between God and us alone and not involve an innocent third party.

The Bible says there is no third party; Jesus was no bystander accidentally caught up in our mess: God the Father and Jesus the Son were so close in this matter that they were one. Jesus agreed to this. He knew that in his hour of glory, he was to be lifted up on a cross, providing the means by which all people could be drawn to him and be pardoned and forgiven. "God so loved the world that he gave his one and only Son." God paid the price himself.

The way of love

To illustrate that God is taking the punishment himself, think of God as a faithful wife whose husband has been cheating on her. How should the woman feel about her husband living with another woman? Should she be serene and indifferent to his behaviour? If she is not hurt and angry, then either the relationship was a sham or she is morally and emotionally dysfunctional.

One day the husband turns up genuinely sorry and repentant. He says: "Please forgive me. I messed up but want to come back to you: will you have me back? I have ended the other relationship because I want to repair things with you. It is you I love."

What should his wife say? How about: "Oh yeah, sure, no problem – I hardly noticed you were gone"? That would surely be amoral and indifferent and indicate that no real love or passion towards her husband ever existed. Should she remain angry and divorce him for everything she can get? The law would be on her side and she would not be unjust or unreasonable in doing so, but it would not be a healing of the wound, rather it would be more like an amputation. Although she is hurt and angry, she still loves him.

There is another way, but it is costly. It's the way of love and mercy and isn't easy or sentimental and a price needs to be paid. True love has the power not to ignore hurt, but to absorb it. Rather than allow the relationship to be destroyed by the offence, this is what the woman does: she says to her estranged husband as he stands on her doorstep: "I do still love you and I will have you back." Does that seem a little easy? Does his forgiveness seem to come a little cheaply? Surely, there should be a price for that man's adultery. There is. The husband knows his wife has paid the price for his forgiveness. He knows that the cost of his acceptance is the pain, humiliation and anguish his wife must endure in order to accept him back and make the relationship work. He knows that this pain, humiliation and anguish will be felt by her for the rest of her life. The way of love is costly, not cheap.

Tough love

That's what Jesus did on the cross!
He chose the way of love. God is rightly
angry at our sin, which is a continuous
lifestyle of hurtful disloyalty towards him
and defiles all that he had made and
cherishes. Yet there on the cross we see
Jesus coming to terms with our sin by
taking it on himself. It was as if Jesus
absorbed all our appalling
unfaithfulness, pride, jealousy, envy and
bitterness into his own divine self on the
cross.

That was the real agony of the cross:
Jesus   who had never sinned and
who hated sin – took the filth and
degradation of your sin and mine into his
own divine self and experienced the
anguish of being separated from his
Father as he bore the hellish punishment
we deserve. That's why Jesus died.

When Jesus fully paid the price for sin
on the cross and was ready to give up

his spirit and die, he said, "It is finished" (John 19:30). Not: "I am finished." The word translated *finished* means "completed". It is the word a student would use having sat their last exam, or someone who has just paid the last instalment of their mortgage. There is nothing more to do, nothing more to pay: "Finished." Sin has been paid for, death has been defeated and the powers of hell conquered, *finished*.

Our response

Do you realise how you have angered and offended God's holy love for you? Yet his love for you is so great that he is willing to have you back. He offers you forgiveness, love and acceptance. Jesus is willing to offer you a fresh start, with all the guilt removed. In addition to taking our sin, God is able to clothe us in Jesus' righteousness – so that he can look on us without being offended by our sin. He loves us so much that he will commit himself to you today and for eternity as your Saviour and friend.

A few years ago I spoke at a university and after giving a talk on the death of Jesus, I was confronted by a student called Helen who felt that the concept of Jesus taking her place had become even more confusing after hearing my talk. I swallowed my pride and gave her a book called *The Cross of Christ* by John Stott (IVP). A couple of weeks later I received this email from a friend of hers:

" Dear Richard,

Helen has been devouring the book she was given. Last Thursday she called me to tell me that finally "it's all clicked" and she can understand why Jesus died for her, and was able to accept it for herself. Since then she's had this big smile on her face that she just can't shake, and she tells me, half-embarrassed, that she's full of joy! Praise God for opening her eyes. Helen's already had some great conversations with her housemate explaining the gospel and sharing her new faith, and is excited to get stuck into church. **"**

Your response

If you would like to investigate further the key evidence for Christianity visit www.bethinking.org/booklets and choose from a variety of talks and articles.

If it has "all clicked" for you, and you understand how you can be forgiven and accepted by God through what Jesus has achieved on the cross, and if you are willing to turn away from self-rule and make Jesus your Lord and God, I would encourage you to do exactly what Helen did. Accept it, tell others and get stuck into a local church. You can begin by praying this prayer:

Prayer

"

I thank you that Jesus Christ died on the cross for me. I realise that my sin is so serious that it took Jesus to die in my place, to honour your just character and to pay the price for my sin.

Lord God,

I admit that I have lived independently of you and have offended your love and provoked your anger with my proud, selfish attitude to you and all that you have made.

I realise that you are too holy and good to simply overlook my sin. Thank you that you loved me so much you were willing to give your only Son to die in my place.

I acknowledge that Jesus willingly laid down his life for me, bearing the punishment my sin deserves and that he now offers me the forgiveness I don't deserve.

I now turn away from everything that is

wrong in my life and ask you to forgive me by virtue of who Jesus is and what he achieved on the cross.

Please send the Spirit of Jesus to live in me – to renew me and help me to be a follower of Jesus from this day on and for the rest of my life.

Amen.

If you have prayed this prayer, speak to a Christian friend or go to our website www.bethinking.org/booklets and email us using "Contact us".